It was this spot on 18th July 1644 that nothing happened

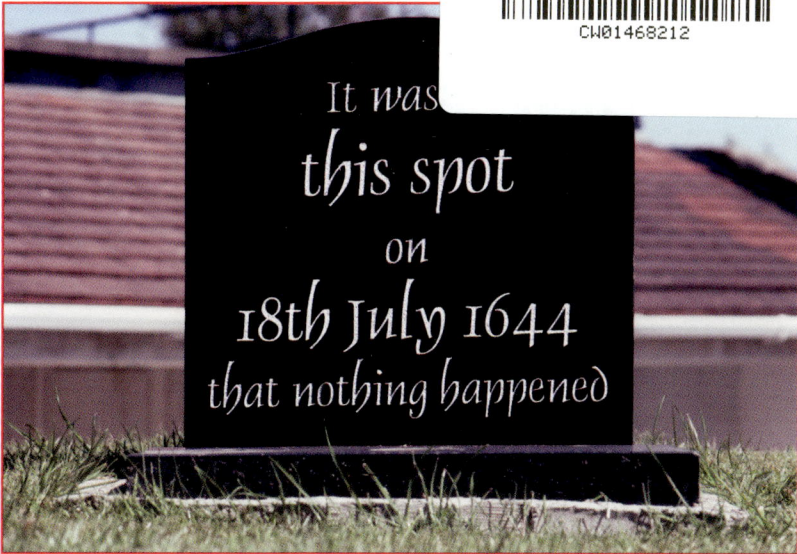

THE LITTLE BOOK OF MANX JOKES

Loaghtan Books
Caardee
Dreemskerry Hill
Maughold
Isle of Man
IM7 1BE

Typesetting and origination by
Loaghtan Books

Printed and bound by
Short Run Press

Published by Loaghtan Books

www.loaghtanbooks.com

First published: October 2025

ISBN: 978 1 908060 47 1

For Suzanne Curphey
Whose idea this was
And therefore whose fault it is!

Rear cover: Weather forecasting stone, Salmon Lake Centre, Laxey

Title page: At Port-e-Vullen, Maughold

Why is the Isle of Man like
the letter T?
They're both in the middle of
water.

Is a Manx cat
the original tailless wonder?

Occasionally ships run aground
on the Manx shore. One carrying
dark purple dye leaked and its
entire crew was marooned.

Did you hear about the runaway
horse tram?
It's a tale of whoa!

Why are the Manx so good at sports?
Because they're always
a step ahead.

Do *TT* winners
Manximise their potential?

The timetable of the Isle of
Man Steam Railway Co. has to
be exact to make use of the
passing loops.
It's steam work.

Could Laxey canaries be
called miner birds?

Want a romantic getaway?
Love is in the Ayre.

What do you call the Isle of Man
wild wallabies when they
get lazy?
Pouch potatoes.

What do you call Langness
when it tells jokes?
A puninsula.

What do Loaghtan sheep say
to each other at Christmas?
Happy Christmas to Ewe!

No man is an island –
except when he's having a bath.

What happens when *TT*
competitors finish racing?
They re-tyre.

The steam train carrying the
sets and costumes for the Gaiety
Theatre had trouble starting.
It had stage freight.

I said to the foreman at Poyllvaaish quarry: 'that's a very big rock'. He looked at it and said: 'boulder' So I said:
'that's a very big rock.'

Can Manx cats be 'cured' by re-tail therapy?

What do you call a lazy flower on the Isle of Man?
Laxey-daisical.

Where do Manx oranges come from?
Peel.

The little café near Bulgham stops serving at the end of the season. They have a closing Dhoon sale.

Snuff the Wind stands on the Manx uplands.
It mines its own business.

An ambitious farmer at Dhoon keeps the wild goats off the Manx Electric Railway line.
He's a goat-getter.

Have you heard the story about Snaefell?
I couldn't get over it.

Billy Connolly took part in the TT.
He rode a Yamahahaha.

Did you know that Father Christmas has a holiday home on the Isle of Man?
It's at Santan

Some boats hit Kitterland, but it takes atoll on them.

We went to the most northerly point of the Isle of Man on Tuesday.
And Wednesday.
AND Thursday.
Ayre we go again.

Why do the Manx excel at the triathlon?
Because it's got three legs.

Peel was delighted to learn that the Steam Packet would be moving its shipping service to the west of the island.
Unfortunately it was just a ferry tale.

There aren't many roads
in the Isle of Man. On the
northern plain it's sometimes
a case of Bride and seek.

The top of Snaefell gives you
snow better view.
It's peak perfection.

Participants in the Isle of
Man's annual Parish Walk must
make Manximum effort.

The Manx fishermen tried to explain
their problems to the Department
of Environment, Food and
Agriculture (DEFA), but the
politicians weren't listening.
They needed herring aids.

To get harmony in Tynwald you must get the Keys in order.

Why is it called Chicken Rock? Because Chicken Dwayne Johnson would be silly.

The Isle of Man College offers:
A sandwich course in catering
A day release course in probation
and
A créche course for nannies.

Calf Sound?
Moo!

To celebrate his retirement, one of the presenters on Manx Radio went home from Douglas by steam train. It was the ex-press.

What's a Dhoon kid's favourite song?
'Row, row, row your goat.'
His parents prefer 'I goat you babe'.

Every year the Isle of Man
railways take on seasonal staff.
They're train-ees.

Who are the most popular
actors on the Isle of Man?
Kirk and Michael Douglas.

Why are Manx cats bad liars?
They have no tail to tell.

The northern part of the
Isle of Man experienced a
record-breaking 18 hours of
sunshine.
It was an Ayre fryer.

Most of the pigs on the Isle
of Man live in one place.
Oink-an.

Some tourists were visiting
Castle Rushen and asked a guide
whether there were any ghosts.
'Don't worry', said the guide,
'I've been here for 300 years and
I've never seen any...'

I asked about Snaefell.
It's so fantastic I had to
summit up.

Why didn't the motorbike
race in the TT ?
Because it was two tyred.

Why did fastcraft Manannan
cross the Irish Sea?
To get to the other tide.

Manx cats don't need GPS
they use Cat-Nav.

What's a TT fan's least
favourite coffee?
Flat white.

An Englishman an Irishman and a
Scotsman went into a Manx pub.
A notice said 'no jokes allowed'.
It was the Bar-rule.

The Isle of Man Steam Railway Co.
insists that smoking is not allowed.
It reduces Pullman-ary complaints.

Sometimes Laxey Woollen Mill
produces green tweed.
It's lovat first sight.

What do you call Elon Musk
on Douglas beach?
A basking shark.

Visiting the Chasms I asked
my mate:
'Canyon believe those views?'

The supporters of different
TT bikes confuse me.
What's the greater traction?

St Germain Cathedral's
bellringers were prosecuted by
the Noise Abatement Society.
They lost on a peal.

Heron & Brearley have tied pubs.
Does this make them
trussed houses?

Locomotive *Maitland* failed at
Port Erin.
It had a bad coal-d.

The horse tram has tried to
economise by employing someone
who is half man and half horse.
The *Isle* of *Man Examiner* made it
a centaur spread.

Manx cats don't have tails
so they end abruptly.

The priest spoke to the
congregation in Peel Cathedral with
knitted brows, the odd serge of
emotion, heart-felt sympathy and
just a touch of flannel.
I could tell he was a
man of the cloth.

At King William's School my
son had A for effort and E for
achievement.
It's why he failed in spelling.

How do the important
Manx families rent Castle Rushen?
HeirBnB

She used to go to the Palace
Casino to play roulette but
disliked the colour red.
That made her bête noir.

The single father of some of the
kids at Dhoon advertised that
he needed a nanny.

The Tynwald choir is
never off Key.

Motormen (drivers) on the Manx Electric Railway can't be electrocuted.
They don't conduct.

What do Manx cats think about their homeland?
It's purr-fect.

A pessimist, an optimist and a realist look along the tunnel of the Great Laxey Mines Railway.
The pessimist sees a long dark tunnel. The optimist sees a light at the end of the tunnel. The realist sees that the light is an oncoming train.
The driver sees three idiots standing on the track.

Maughold lighthouse is actually very heavy.

One of the people who work
for Manx National Heritage
fell off Peel Castle.
He was de-moat-ed.

What sort of bike did Father
Christmas ride in the *TT*?
A Holly Davidson.

The Lieutenant Governor
used to live in Castle Rushen.
In a manor of speaking.

A buggane lives at Ballagorry
under the only over-bridge on
the tram line.
He's the Manx Electric
Railway's arch enemy.

Why did the Chicken Rock?
She had a set of drumsticks.

Conductors on the Manx Electric Railway eventually become drivers.
It's a tram-endous opportunity.
If they don't get side-tracked.

A famous writer moved to live near Castletown.
He had a Study in Scarlett.

How long did it take to build Castle Rushen?
A fortnight.

The Isle of Man Steam Railway Co. carries far more passengers than goods.
It's hard to keep a freight face.

Have you heard about the Manx confectioner?
He sold Kelly-babies.

Manx wallabies can be coaxed out
of hiding by playing them music.
They like hip hop.
Or hopera.

Spooyt Vane?
Wonderfall.

We walked the Raad ny Foillan
around the north of the
Isle of Man.
It was Ayre-mazing.

To get to work some of
the Snaefell Mountain
Railway drivers have to get
up at the track of dawn.

How many Manx does it take
to change a lightbulb?
None.
The Manx don't like change...

A Member of the House of Keys objected to the building of the Sulby Reservoir.
His argument didn't hold water.

The Isle of Man Steam Railway Co. doesn't have express trains.
They're slowcomotives.

What are the Bulgham goats called? Hillbillies.

Why are people from Colby most trustworthy?
Because they're on the Level.

The 8 o'clock Manx Electric Railway tram was ahead of schedule.
It left at twenty to wait.

A Laxey hairdresser was arrested.
She'd been grooming miners.

The trammers (tram horses)
are well trained but still have
to pass a test before working
in earnest.
Most get a hay-plus.

The drivers of the Isle of Man
Steam Railway Co. trains are
known for their engine-uity.

Why do seagulls live at sea?
Because if they lived in
Ramsey Bay
they'd be bagels.

Successful Members of the
House of Keys unlock their full
potential.

We like to take the Manx Electric
Railway tram home.
But we have to give it back.

Occasionally an Isle of Man
Steam Railway Co. train fails.
It takes one to no-one.

What did the Irish Sea say to
the Manx coast?
Nothing, it just waved.

A new rider in the TT got lost
and ended up in Sulby River.
He was riding a motor pike.

What did the fisherman say when
he saw Langness lighthouse?
'There she glows.'

What do you call a snake on
the Isle of Man?
Lost.

Have you heard about the Loaghtan
sheep which was lost on Snaefell?
It was found at Creg-ny-baa.

Going from the rocks of
Spanish Head to the sands
of Blue Point is a whole
different dune-iverse.

The Great Laxey Mine is
totally ore-inspiring.

Why do the trammers pull the
horse trams?
Because they're too heavy to carry.

Where do Manx basking
sharks go on holiday?
Finland.

An Indian Restaurant in Douglas
created a delicious new dish of
unleaved bread and spicy meat.
They called it the Isle of Naan.

A buggane, the Phynoderee and
seagod Manannan walked into a
Manx bar.
They were in the wrong joke.

The Manx coast is amazing.
You have to seas the day.

Driving the train between Port Soderick and Ronaldsway is more difficult than it steams.

Having caught nothing, the Port St Mary fishing fleet went to an audiologist. They had herring loss.

Have you heard about the Laxey business man? He was a big wheel.

Fynoderee gin? No Druidale.

Why does the Harbour Master radio the Steam Packet boats in Manx? Because they're not on the English Channel.

The Isle of Man has a shortage of dentists, so the Manx government organised a tooth ferry.

It's rare for the Douglas Bay Tramway to run after dark, but when they do the trams are harnessed to nightmares.

An Indian restaurant has taken over the little café on the Manx Electric Railway line near Bulgham.
It specialises in Chicken Dhoona.

What do you call the Meayll Circle? A wheel barrow.

We'd planned to go to Dog Mills but ran out of time.
We had to cur-tail it.

A visitor looking at Manx kippers commented that smoking was bad for you.
'It's OK'. the shopkeeper assured him, 'they've been cured'.

We went to Port St Mary with everyone else.
We gave in to pier pressure.

People say their Manx cats talk to them.
It's mews to me.

Two drivers were seen fighting over the charging points in Market Place, Ramsey.
Witnesses were shocked as one socketed the other. Police will amp up patrols.

Ballaterson Farm bought a pedigree ram and, because he was so expensive, called him Bill. He had his own special pen. It was the Bill-tup area.

Most of the Manx fishingboats fish for scallops. They're hard of herring.

Howard on Manx Radio is always threatening to eat his pants. Many a true word is spoken ingest.

If life on the Isle of Man seems rosy, it's not a pigment of the imagination.

Baldwin – PR for hairloss

Four coachloads of unexpected passengers arrived at Douglas railway station but the staff kept calm and carriaged on.

What do you call musicians at Cashel-yn-Ard?
A rock band.

Head to Gansey for some vitamin sea.
I shore will.

People living on Lamb Hill complained that they weren't in the film.
Their neighbours on Kimmeragh Road explained: 'it's West Bride Story'.

What did the Irish Sea say to the Baldwin River?
You can run but you can't tide.

My husband uses the Manx Electric Railway a lot but never gets into trouble.

He has a get out of rail free card.

The House of Keys and the Legislative Council are trapped in a warzone. Who survives? The Isle of Man.

What do you get when you cross the Dhoo and the Glass?

Wet feet.

As the Tynwald building is called The Wedding Cake, does that make the Isle of Man a dessert island?

The Curragh Wildlife Park was recruiting new keepers. They needed good koala-fications.

One customer of Laxey Woollen Mill has just one hobby, that of collecting waistcoats. He only has one per suit.

The man who runs Laxey Flour Mill is a great musician. He's a Glen Miller.

A Manx farmer supplemented his income by making Nickies (a type of Manx boat) in his barn. Sails are going through the roof.

What did the holidaymaker say when leaving the Isle of Man? 'Manx for the memories'!

The Isle of Man. A view-tiful place.